Doesn't Anyone Blush Anymore?

Manis Friedman

edited by JS Morris

B A I S
CHANA
PRESS

A Division of Community Education Organization

ב״ה

DOESN'T ANYONE BLUSH ANYMORE?
Copyright © 1990 by Bais Chana Tapes, a division of Community
Education Organization, and JS Morris. All rights reserved. Printed in the United
States of America. No part of this book may be used or reproduced in any manner
whatsoever without written permission except in the case of brief quotations embod-
ied in critical articles and reviews. For information address Bais Chana Press,
Community Education Organization, 3208 W. Lake Street, Suite 770,
Minneapolis, Minnesota 55416.

FIRST BAIS CHANA PRESS PAPERBACK EDITION
PUBLISHED IN 1996

Library of Congress Cataloging-in-Publication Data
Friedman, Manis.

    Doesn't anvone blush anymore? / Manis Friedman.

        p. cm.

    1. Sex—Religious aspects—Judaism. 2. Judaism. I. Title.
BM720.S4F75 1990
    296.3'8566—dc20

89-45992
CIP

MCN 10 9 8 7 6 5 4

More Advance Praise for Manis Friedman and
Doesn't Anyone Blush Anymore?

"The strength of the book is its unabashed celebration
and reverence for marriage. Rabbi Friedman avoids
much of the hackneyed and trite pop psychology that
surrounds us." —Edward Hoffman, Ph.D., clinical
psychologist and author

"Manis Friedman is a major force on the contemporary
moral scene. His book will change lives." —Allan Leicht,
Emmy Award–winning writer and producer

"Friedman is the lamp lighting a spiritual journey for
thousands, [a] man revered worldwide as a scholar,
speaker, and counselor, who is noted as much for his
sense of humor as his intensity." —Kim Ode,
Minneapolis Star Tribune

"Manis Friedman is hypnotic, compelling, deep, and very
appealing. He never fails to give me a great deal to
think about." —Velvl W. Greene, Ph.D., director, Center
of Medical Ethics, Ben-Gurion University, Israel

"Drawing on the accumulated wisdom of over three
thousand years, master storyteller Rabbi Friedman offers
startlingly practical advice into nearly every facet of
human existence." —Peter Himmelman, songwriter,
recording artist

"Friedman is an excellent communicator, and a prophet
for an ethic-sick generation." —Reverend John D.
Gilmore, St. Paul Area Council of Churches

"Rabbi Friedman taught me to be concerned more with the needs of the soul than those of the body, to discover that the truly superior people are those with spiritual and ethical integrity—not just wealth and good looks."
—Ilana Harkavi, president, Il Makiage International Salon, and author of *I Can Make You Beautiful*

"Manis Friedman practices the difficult art of taking ancient truths and making them relevant in today's world." —Michael Kelberer, *The Phoenix: Recovery, Renewal, Growth*

"In the past, there was an attitude: 'Thou shalt, thou shalt not,' but what Rabbi Friedman is teaching is welcoming, warm, and joyous. It's something to behold, how people respond to him." —Rachael Silman, Minneapolis Public Schools guidance counselor

"A master teacher and a much-sought-after speaker. Friedman combines spiritual life and everyday living with a vigorous intellectualism." —*The Highland Villager*

"You may not always like Rabbi Friedman's answers, but they will make you think . . . and think . . . and think." —Sarah C. Rosenthal, New York City public relations consultant

"I wept when I read *Doesn't Anyone Blush Anymore?* And I'm a Congregationist! Rabbi Friedman touched me where I needed and wanted to be touched. An incredibly valuable book in the struggle for intimacy." —Frank Kinikin, award-winning writer, and producer of *Blood Harvest*

Dedicated to

Rebbetzin Chaya Moussia Schneerson

of blessed memory

Contents